To Elisabeth

with love

from

malcolm

Christmas 1976.

Pools and Terraces

HOUSE & GARDEN

GUIDE TO LANDSCAPING AND FURNISHING

by Gail Heathwood

COLLINS – LONDON AND GLASGOW
IN ASSOCIATION WITH THE CONDÉ NAST PUBLICATIONS LTD.

Published by WM. COLLINS SONS & CO. LTD.
LONDON AND GLASGOW
in association with THE CONDÉ NAST PUBLICATIONS LTD.
COPYRIGHT © 1974 THE CONDÉ NAST PUBLICATIONS LTD.

ISBN 0 00 435089 8

Printed in Great Britain by Wm. Collins Sons & Co. Ltd.

Contents

Acknowledgements: The following photographers are represented: Jacques
Bachmann, Morley Baer, Gérard Bellot, Carlo de Benedetto, Jacques Boucher,
Emmet Bright, Harold Davis, Durel, Richard Einzig, Geneviève, Grigsby,
Guillat, Patrick Heyworth, Horst, Marc Lacoix, Lautman, Frank Lotz Miller,
Dearborn Massar, Maris-Selem, Mulas, Michel Nahmias, Primois/Pinto, Norman
Parkinson, Karl H Riek, Henk Snoek, Ezra Stoller, Michel Wickham,
Ray Williams, Tom Yee

Introduction

It may well be that swimming, as an activity, began out of man's necessity to gather the fruits of the sea. It is certainly true that man almost immediately discovered its pleasurable and beneficial aspects. Since that day no sport, hobby, or recreational pursuit has had such a widespread popularity – as history readily shows: in ancient Egypt, Greece, and Rome immersion was a matter of more than mere bathing.

Now, as urban overcrowding forces us further and further from our coastlines, we must substitute man-made facilities for those provided by nature – in the same way, in fact, as civilizations long before ours. The daily dip has become part of the routine of more families than ever before as domestic swimming pools, their efficiency guaranteed and their cost reduced by technical expertise, have become more accessible to an increasingly affluent society. Today it is estimated that more than 50,000 new private swimming pools are built in the developed countries of the world each year. Apart from the health and recreational benefits to the individual, a pool serves also as a family-and-friends gathering place – ideal because it brings people together in the most relaxed and unconstrained conditions possible. As an addition to your property, it is a bonus – both in terms of an attractive garden or internal feature and in the value of the property to which it adds.

A terrace, either one surrounding the pool or any other, is a logical first step in extending the scope of a house; a link, if you like, between the house and the garden, neither one nor the other, but enhancing both. Adding a terrace means creating a second environment for the pursuit of everyday activities, providing a choice of atmospheres in which to eat, relax and entertain. The ultimate success of these projects depends to a large extent on your initial knowledge of them; you must know how to approach pool and terrace building if these features are to become a fully integrated part of your environment.

Hence this book, which is a practical but not confusingly technical guide to how to locate, construct, and landscape; how to heat, light, maintain, and furnish both pool and terrace as inexpensively or as luxuriously as you like. As a comprehensive step-by-step reference, those who are about to move a part of their living outdoors will find it a valuable storehouse of decorative ideas and practical suggestions.

A pool built as part of the living complex is ideal for family entertainment and exercise. A multiplicity of balconies emphasizes the outdoor feeling. Steps lead down to the terrace with ample space both for play and a sitting-out area. Design by David A Smith

A practical look at pool building

Domestic swimming pools are either excavated – 'in the ground', or 'below ground' – or constructed primarily to be sited above ground, although some 'above ground' pools can also be partially or fully sunken.

The traditional way to build a swimming pool is below ground, and because of the excavation involved, and for other reasons as well, it is expensive. Once the excavation for a below ground pool has been made, there are numerous ways to complete it. In the block construction method, a concrete floor is first poured. This is used as a footing for hollow reinforced concrete blocks which are filled with poured concrete in situ. Alternatively, an inner and outer shell of concrete blocks or bricks can be filled with steel reinforced concrete. In the poured construction method, the floor is again poured first and used as a base for walls of reinforced concrete to be poured between shutters and compacted by vibration. In the Gunite method (the fastest way to build a concrete pool) a cement and sand aggregate is sprayed at pressure onto a steel mesh reinforcement pre-shaped to fit the excavation. A concrete mixture can also be hand-packed onto a pre-shaped reinforced 'cage'. In both these methods, walls and floor are built in one continuous operation.

Below ground pools can also be constructed of steel or aluminium, usually in pre-fabricated panel form, lined with a flexible, waterproof vinyl or butyl liner, fabricated to fit the contours of the retaining material exactly. Pre-fabricated concrete blocks can also be used in conjunction with a flexible pool liner, and pre-fabricated fibre-glass shapes, packed into the excavation with sand and concrete, are becoming increasingly popular for below ground use, although they are as yet relatively expensive. With any of these construction methods, the cost of below ground pools can be reduced by partial as opposed to full excavation, the excavated soil then being used to bank the surrounds to the height of the exposed walls.

Above ground pools, generally a more economical form of construction, are of pre-fabricated metal – steel or aluminium – or of specially treated timber, assembled in situ and finished with a flexible, watertight liner. Landscaping the surrounds of an above ground pool tends to be more difficult, and sometimes more expensive, than the landscaping of a sunken pool, a factor which should be considered when making cost comparisons.

How to choose an appropriate pool

Your decision will be influenced by three main factors – size, cost, and location. Usage will affect size, size will affect cost, size and cost might be

Irregular pool set within a rough stone terrace is shielded from the wind by a dense belt of trees, and low spreading shrubs have been planted in the terrace to give it a more natural appearance. The roof of the pool house, with its changing rooms and small kitchen, slopes right down to the ground, providing additional shelter

Perfectly simple rectangular pool below a steep bank that shelters it from prevailing winds. The small pavilion is changing room and equipment store for both pool and tennis court

affected by location, and location might be affected by climate, terrain, the location of existing services, and local authority regulations. Before any final decision is made, therefore, each of these factors must be considered separately and in relation to each other.

Usage

Determine first where the pool will fit into the pattern of family entertainment. In an adult, or verging on adult household, it is probable that the pool will not be expected to contend with the same intense activity as it would in a family with several young children. Such is the case, too, when children are away at school for a large part of the year, or if alternative recreational facilities are offered, such as tennis courts. On the other hand, if yours is a gregarious family, and it can thus be assumed that one or two extra bodies will generally be enjoying pool hospitality, aim for a size which will accommodate a mixed dozen – toddlers through to adults – in harmony and safety. If the pool is intended for year-round use, budget at the outset for a pool enclosure (or make it an indoor pool) and adequate heating and lighting.

Size

A good size for an average family, of, say, four or five, is a pool 40 ft long by 16 ft wide (or its volumetric equivalent in whatever shape you choose). The smallest pool worth owning is around 20 ft by 10 ft, and bear in mind that any pool, for aesthetic as well as practical reasons, should be approximately half as wide as it is long.

Shape

There are virtually no limitations on what shape a swimming pool can be, though your choice might be governed to some extent by the available location. As an alternative to a rectangular pool, or a rectangle with a bay at one end for decoration or as a special shallow children's bay, you can have a circular pool, or any variation of a circle, or a free-form pool – kidney shapes, kite shapes and so on. Note, however, that a rectangle is cheaper to construct than a circular or free-form pool.

Cost

A general rule of thumb, in relating the cost of installing a pool to the improved value of your property, is that if a professionally built pool does not exceed 10% of the total property value, its cost will be recovered. The cost of the average-sized pool referred to above, in a conventional below ground construction, including excavation, filtration and heating equipment and basic surrounds, will be in the vicinity of £4,000. The things which will add to the cost will be construction difficulties presented by an unusual site, an elaborate shape, and special finishes, equipment and accessories. Above ground pools range from around £450 for a basic, pre-fabricated, do-it-yourself kit, up to £2,000 for an above ground pool installed with heating, lighting, accessories and basic landscaping.

Location

The pool should be as near to the house as possible, close to water and

Curved pool with a small paddling area at one end. The three steps across the neck enclose the shallow end for additional safety, and over the farther end a lifebelt is hung on the wall

electricity supplies, suitably sited for drainage, and in the flattest possible spot to avoid excavation difficulties. It should be in the sunniest place you can find which meets those requirements, and away from trees and shrubbery so that vegetation will not add to the problem of keeping the pool clean. If there are small children to be watched, then the shallow end is logically placed nearest the house, but at the same time, the prevailing wind should move surface debris towards the end of the pool in which the skimmer or other surface filter is located. Soil and natural drainage conditions play an important part in the long term efficiency of the pool and are an important siting factor, and there may be certain building regulations to which you must conform. Indoor pools, or those which are built half indoors and half out, should be well insulated so that the rest of the house is not affected by the continually moist air which surrounds them, or by excessive noise, and they should have exits to both the house proper and the outside.

In practice, however, although it will minimize costs and problems to stick as closely as possible to these directives, modern attitudes to pool architecture and design and current construction methods indicate that a certain amount of flexibility in siting one's pool is not only desirable, but also possible. For example, whether you site the pool within visible distance of the house might depend on the extent to which it is to be an entity in itself. If it is to be a complete entertainment/health centre, with sauna, games room, dining and even separate cooking facilities, it may be desirable for it to have a different character to the house proper; if so, it would be best located where one is not visible from the other. On the other hand, if you want the pool to be a physical extension of your house, it will need to be architecturally in keeping with the appearance of your house even if this means that design and construction ingenuity must overcome an awkward site.

Essentially, you may assume that if you have a particular reason for wanting your pool in a particular place, there will be either a design or a structural practice which will enable you to do just that. As for the specific requirements of local building authorities, any professional pool contractor will know what these are. And before he commences construction, the contractor you employ will certainly have the plans approved by the local authority.

Once you have considered all of the foregoing factors, you will then be in a position to decide, in conjunction with the contractor you engage, on the type of pool which is best suited to your needs. At this point, it might be appropriate to offer a few words of advice on choosing a contractor. In comparison with other forms of domestic building, the construction of swimming pools is a young industry. As almost all contractors will tell you, they are learning all the time. Unfortunately, there are some who do not study hard enough before their board goes up, and it is the inexperienced contractor whom you must avoid to be guaranteed a trouble-free result for your money. So before you choose, check that the contractor you intend using is either a member of his trade association, or that he has a satisfactory reason for not being a member. Look at other pools he has constructed, and check whether their owners are completely satisfied; learn as much as you can, so that you can follow intelligently each step as the construction of the pool proceeds.

The order of construction

If you are having a below ground pool installed, the first thing which will take place is the excavation of the pool cavity. This will take only a day or so under normal conditions. (As well as unexpected difficulties in terrain, abnormal conditions will also include periods of bad weather – rain and frost are the arch enemies of the pool contractor, and most work seasonally, at an extremely fast pace, to complete their obligations before the wet season.)

If the construction method used involves the preliminary laying of a concrete floor, the contractor should at this point call on the services of a chartered structural or civil engineer to determine how thick the floor must be. This varies with the prevailing site and soil conditions, as well as the size of the pool, and each case can only be determined individually. Normally a concrete floor will be from four to nine inches thick. The penalties of guesswork here can be enormous, for if it is incorrect, the whole structure might float, the walls and floor might eventually crack,

Built out to overlook Lake Como this terrace has a commanding view. The harsh effect of rectangular design has been softened by the curved corners of the pool and by the plants in the retaining wall

The shallow pool in this enclosed terrace is an integral part of the paved area that surrounds the house. It is overlooked from the cantilevered living-room windows. The opposite end is apsidal with room for children to run around during sailing activities. Design by Keith Ingham

or any one of a number of other disasters occur. To lay the concrete floor, the earth must be accurately levelled, and a base of standard 'beach', a mixture of sand and gravel, laid first. A most important inclusion in the floor of any below ground swimming pool is a hydrostatic relief valve, which is the stabilizing device designed to relieve external water pressures from the pool shell, and maintain the equilibrium of the shell once the pool is filled. It is connected to the base of the sump outlet through which the main flow of water passes to the recirculating pump, filter and heater.

Next come the walls, and after the walls, the pre-formed coping or overhung edge around the top of the pool. At the same time, drainage, filter and heating systems will be installed in pre-determined locations. The inner surfacing of the pool is the next step. In formed concrete pools, the concrete must first be rendered waterproof with two coats of sand and cement screed. The most frequently used surfacing for pools, and in terms of its durability one of the most economical, is marbelite. This is a mixture of white marble chips and dust mixed with white cement and must be applied by a skilled operator if it is to be successful. A waterproof paint can be used as an alternative, although it requires more intensive maintenance to remain attractive and clean. White paint will turn ordinary water blue when the pool is filled, and this is the most usual colour to choose. Pale blue also gives an attractive result, but green is best avoided. Of course, there is nothing to say you cannot paint a pool interior any colour which takes your fancy, and black is sometimes used with dramatic effect, but before you go to extremes, you should be sure that the effect you achieve will be the one you envisaged.

Undoubtedly the most satisfactory material with which to line a pool is frost-proof ceramic tile, as once installed, it needs virtually no attention for the remainder of the pool's life. However, tile is also the most expensive lining medium, and can add as much as £2,000 to the completed cost of the pool.

Whatever you use, there should be a six inch band of tile between the coping and the lining proper, as the water level line is prone to the formation of scum, which might stain any other surface but tile. The most recent innovation in permanent pool lining is the use of fibreglass reinforced plastic, usually sprayed on in liquid form and allowed to set. It has many advantages, but is as yet fairly expensive. Most surfacing requires a two week drying/settling period before the pool can be filled.

If your pool is to have a flexible liner, vinyl is the best choice. It will be a heavy .02 gauge, and is most practical in pale blue or turquoise. Vinyl liners are also available in white, but tend to show dirty marks more clearly than other colours. The liner will be high-frequency welded exactly to the shape of the pool, and under normal conditions, has an excellent life expectancy with few problems likely to be encountered along the way. Ultra-violet rays from sunlight are the vinyl liner's worst enemy, but most are surface treated with a special substance to increase resistance. Butyl sheeting is sometimes used for pool liners, but it must be overpainted with chlorinated rubber or a similar substance if white or blue is required in preference to the natural black in which it is sold.

Once the pool itself has been completed, its surrounds must be properly engineered before they can be landscaped. As this requires quite a deal of technical expertise, most contractors will undertake the basic construction as part of the job. Aesthetically, too, this is desirable, as pool and terrace should be designed as an entity. A 'dry joint' is installed between the pool and its surrounds, to prevent moisture seepage. Backfilling or the replacement of displaced soil around the pool is best done at a rate of $1\frac{1}{2}$in a time, hydraulically tamped between each application until the required level is reached. (Backfilling is usually commenced as the walls are built, rather than after.) This ensures that the soil remains solid, and will not shift under the pressure of normal erosion: the same principle, more or less, as that employed in road-laying. The surrounds should gently slope away from the pool, so that surface water will not drain into it and cause contamination. A drain installed at one or more corners of the pool surround will also help the run-off of surface water. The actual landscaping features of the pool surrounds will be fully discussed in a later chapter. It is sufficient to say here that care should be taken to see that the surfacing immediately adjacent to the pool edge is non-slip, for obvious safety reasons.

As a general rule, the installation of a below ground outdoor pool will take from two to six weeks from excavation to completion, and above ground pools can be installed in anything from a day to a week, with perhaps a little extra time allowed for special landscaping where necessary. Indoor pools will, of course, take longer, not only because of the construction of the shelter which contains them (or the conversion of an existing structure, such as garage or basement), but also because they present special technical problems, mostly to do with heating. Trapped warm air, which can come from both room and water heating causes condensation, and special methods and equipment will be necessary to prevent this becoming a problem. Other special types of pools – children's pools, diving pools, hydrotherapy pools – need special consideration as well, which may

Small pool and timber boarded outdoor dining area lie alongside the house with access through sliding doors. The narrow terrace runs the length of the house and all major rooms open onto it. Design by James Parr

require extra time. Each 'special' must be treated individually, and it is not possible in a general outline of pool construction to include specific, accurate information about them. It is enough to note here that special additions can make an ordinary pool into an exciting outdoor complex, if usage warrants and budget allows.

In the design and construction of a swimming pool, there are two other important aspects it is as well to consider at the outset. They are accessories, and safety, and since the two are frequently related, it is best that they be considered together.

Articles which come under the heading of pool accessories are steps, ladders, diving boards, slides, windows, floats, ropes, jumpboards, underwater lights and games equipment.

If steps are to be recessed in the pool wall (not viable with flexible liner pools), they should be moulded, non-slip plastic, or have a non-slip glazed surface, with grooved treads and a handrail. They should be so designed as to avoid any trap for the bather's limbs. The alternative, overhanging stainless steel steps implanted in the pool edge, contain the required safety features in their intrinsic design. Stainless steel steps are available for both corners and straight edges so that it is possible to adhere to the safety rule of one set of steps for every 75 ft of perimeter without the use of special designs. Special ladders, designed so that no part of the structure touches the pool interior, are available for flexible liner pools.

Diving boards come in a great variety of styles and materials, and the type you choose will depend on the size, shape and depth of your pool. To present a guideline, the average rectangular domestic pool with a maximum water depth of 8 ft is best suited by a deck level board of approximately 10 ft length, normally clearing the water by 15 in. In choosing a diving board, the main point to be sure of is that the ratio between the length and spring of the board, and the depth of the water is correct for optimum safety. The same will apply to jumpboards, and to pool slides, when the slope of the slide and the resulting velocity of the person entering the water must be accurately weighed against the depth of the water.

Pool windows are obviously an extravagance unless the view to be had through them is worthwhile, and underwater lights are another extravagance, though well worth it, for there is nothing quite like the calm beauty of underlit water at night. If you intend having either, or both, they should be installed at the initial construction stage, as they are a particularly expensive and sometimes impossible afterthought.

Every pool owner should automatically include life rings and life hooks as part of his standard equipment. If he is fully safety conscious, he will add to those basics every piece of safety equipment he can find, especially if there are young children in the family. Floats, stabilized by connecting waterproof rope, which define the deep from the shallow end of the pool by colour are an excellent idea, and the same goes for one of the various floating pool alarms, usually electrically or battery operated and activated by the slightest movement of water. The best safeguard of all, against straying toddlers and animals (remember, your dog can easily fall in, but he will not be able to get out), especially when the pool is some distance from the house, is a high surrounding fence with a padlocked gate, which can be made attractive with climbing vines and other foliage.

Dramatic indoor pool overlooked from the main living spaces on the upper floor. The pool is shaded and cool in contrast to the sand dunes outside. With internal and external access, the pool has its own complex of changing rooms and sauna. Design by Charles Gwathmey

Ornamental pools

Traditionally, ornamental pools are constructed in concrete or stone, but as with swimming pools, modern technology and materials have initiated swifter and less expensive methods. These days there is scarcely any reason to expend time, energy and money involved in concrete construction of an ornamental pool, when the same effect can be achieved far more easily with one of many pre-fabricated counterparts available. In the main, they come as rigid shapes in fibreglass, smooth or with a simulated rock finish, or as liners in waterproof PVC of some kind. In the simplest terms, you excavate, place the rigid shape or liner in the excavation, landscape the edges, fill

Shallow ornamental pool in a glass-roofed house in Sweden reflects the sky and plants set into the timber floor. The four part roof, operated by a hydraulic mechanism, can open like a lily and expose the whole area to the sky. In winter wooden floor sections cover the pool. Design by Bengt Warne

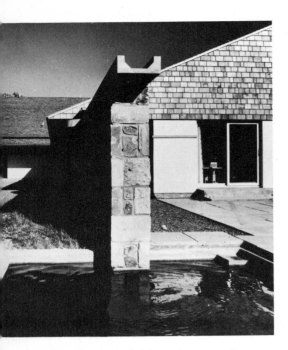

Small pool is fed by rain water from the long sloping roof. The terrace alongside continues across the secluded garden facade of the house. Design by James Morris

Opposite The apparent simplicity of this glass-fronted pool house conceals a comprehensive range of rooms; sitting area, sauna, changing rooms which double as guest-rooms and a small but complete kitchen. Design by Adrian Gale

with water and whatever plants and livestock appeal most. By either method, there is almost no limit to the shapes you can have – the most formal to the most free-form are available.

The methods of installation vary slightly. For the fibreglass shape, you will need to more or less match the excavation. Make sure the shape beds well, and pack it into place solidly with earth. When using a liner, the excavation may be any shape (remember to create ledges and different levels as you go, to allow for the artistic siting of plants later on) for once the liner is placed in the excavation, held by stones at the edges, the pressure of incoming water will mould the liner to the shape of the excavation. Calculate the size of the liner you will need by measuring the length of the pool, and adding twice the deepest depth. Then measure the width, and add twice the deepest depth: for example, an excavation 10 by 8 by 2 ft will need a liner 14 ft by 12 ft. Completion is then a mere matter of bedding the edges firmly with rocks, earth and foliage. Ornamental pools should be placed away from trees and shaded areas, because although the water does not need to be regularly cleaned and filtered as with swimming pools, an excessive build-up of vegetation will eventually make an unpleasant, murky, and smelly pool. Many flowering aquatics, too, need to enjoy an ample supply of light. If you do not want the pool to freeze solid in winter (which will certainly apply if it contains livestock) keep its depth to a minimum 15 in. At maximum it should be around 36 in. For most plants, the depth of soil in the pool will need to be approximately 6 in minimum and the depth of water 4 in. Special containers are available to hold plants underwater so that soil is not distributed over the floor of the pool.

There are many accessories and additions you can use to enhance a basic ornamental pool. If you want moving water, or a stream or waterfall (fibreglass moulds come in both these shapes) or perhaps a fountain, you will need a small pump to circulate the water. In this instance, the pool should not be too far from the mains water supply, as long pipe runs are best avoided. The best kind of pump to buy is electrically operated, with an inbuilt filter and transformer. The transformer reduces the normal household voltage to a much lower, safer level without any loss of power, so that livestock – and even paddling children – are never in danger. One pump is capable of servicing several circulation processes, which can be attached as you acquire them. You can go to the trouble of underlighting an ornamental pool, but in this case, the pool will need to be of concrete, with lights installed during construction. It is hardly worth the extra expense, since a few strategically placed spotlights, or even flares, buried in the surrounding foliage, will have an equally desirable effect. Under ordinary conditions, ornamental pools do not need regular mechanical cleaning and filtering, as an adequate supply of water snails will do the job naturally, and the pool can always be hand cleaned if it gets too dirty. But remember when siting the pool that it will be subject to natural run-off, and should not be placed at the foot of a slope where it will collect silt. If you have young children, always bear in mind, too, that an ornamental pool is as much a potential danger as any other pool, even at a depth of 12 in. Where there is any risk, cover the pool with a wide wire mesh, quite easy to disguise with plants, and removable as the children grow up.

Above left Sheltered on one side by a garden wall and on the other by a tall hedge, a kite-shaped pool with children's paddling area

Left Free-form lines of the pool are reflected by the equally uncompromising lines of the sculpture by David von Schlegel

Above A wedge-shaped pool in the angle of twenty foot high retaining walls. It is on the lowest level of a house built down the side of a wooded hill. Douglas fir boarding around the pool and on the upper terrace is bleached grey. Design by Keith Kroeger and Leonard Perfido

Pools can take on the character of their setting simply by their shape and colour

Top left Meandering rock-bound pool in wooded farmland has a black-painted lining which creates the feeling of a woodland pond. Design by Edward Stone Jr

Bottom left Colours and shapes of surrounding sand dunes are repeated in a pool and deceptively primitive pool house. Design by Paolo Solero

Right Free-form pool in a shaded garden is overhung by an outcrop of natural rock. Pool surrounds are paved with the same simple grey stone

Incorporating a pool into a special
terrace design can produce striking
and unconventional results
Left In keeping with the Moorish
flavour of this terrace in a Tunisian
house, the pool is simply stepped down
one level and contained within the
same solid white concrete walls.
Inflatable plastic cushions add gaiety
and colour
Below Marbelite-lined pool in a simple,
rectangular shape is part of a
geometric design of patches of grass
and different pavings, linking pool
with house

Above The sea seems to roll right onto this large terrace built just above the beach. Wide, shallow steps in the pool lead down gently from the main sitting area to the full depth. On either side of the terrace are high screening walls. Design by Hugh Jackson

Right An L-shaped, seventy five foot long pool that has been made an integral part of the garden design. The liner has been painted dark grey to increase the apparent depth. Design by Kipp Stewart

Above and top right Two views of a
pool near Toulon in France, with the
pool house in the form of a scaled-down
Saracen tower. Upstairs is a small
studio and underneath changing rooms,
a kitchen and shaded terrace. The
rough-hewn timber, dry stone walls
and crazy paving contrast strongly
with the lines of the pool and
contribute to the rustic setting. Design
by Claude Vilgour

Opposite Mediterranean terra-cotta
tiles and rose-covered stucco walls
make a delightful setting for this pool
in Surrey. Design by
Patrick Hayworth
Right A pool in St Tropez, which is
resplendent with a highly original
trompe l'oeil carpet, carried out by
ceramicist Christien Ploix

Two settings that incorporate existing architecture to create a special ambiance

Above Part of a Romanesque cloister surrounds this pool in France, adding interest and shading a terrace

Left A pool built on the site of the winter garden of a Victorian mansion with an imposing row of Victorian pillars running along one side. Design by Michael Manser Associates

Above right The use of old tiles and stone achieves continuity of style with existing architecture in this pool, set into a hillside terrace

Below The white paving of the terrace is emphasized by decorative walls of white lattice work, furniture and umbrella

Above A pool in the limited space of a town house garden. It is divided by glass sliding doors and bridged by a mosaic walkway which leads, via a spiral staircase, to a first floor terrace. Design by Brian Peake

Right The striking lines of this modern loggia and pool, which are built in concrete and timber, are emphasized by the decorative use of modern sculpture and simple but practical plastic seating

Above This greenhouse pool was evolved from an existing hothouse and adjoining potting sheds. It is equipped with barbecue and changing rooms
Left Splendidly domed pool with a circular motif which is repeated in the pool floor. It is built adjacent to the main house
Right Complete recreation centre in a converted barn in Belgium. The pool is heated by an open copper-hooded fire. The room is large enough to lounge about in comfort, as well as providing space for indoor games and barbecue. Natural light floods through large skylights

Swimming pool operation and maintenance

This is a very complex subject, but one with which every pool owner must be concerned, for once his pool is installed, he virtually becomes his own pool janitor. Contractors provide guarantees, and a certain amount of after-sales service, but not, as yet, a regular weekly maintenance service – unfortunately for those to whom such duties fall.

The efficient long term operation of your swimming pool really begins with the excavation. It may be that any number of adverse conditions exist which will not be discovered until a test excavation is made. Amongst these are waterlogged ground, geological faults, soil containing harmful salts. Each of these conditions may require individually tailored solutions, and this is where your contractor's knowledge and experience will be put to the test. However, there are certain standard procedures which he should follow if there is the slightest evidence that any of these conditions exist. With any hard surface pool, it is advisable to equip the sump outlet, built into the lowest point of the floor (this occurs about two thirds of the way down towards the deep end – the pool floor never slopes consistently in one direction, but is always wedged shaped) with a hydrostatic relief valve. This reduces external water pressure by allowing such water to come into the pool, so that it does not float. If conditions are particularly waterlogged, land drains may need to be installed to take the external run off to a lower point, and the outer as well as the inner surface of walls may need to be waterproofed. Where harmful salts are present, a special sulphate-resistant cement should be used, or an isolating coat of bituminous or similar proofing applied.

As well as the sump outlet, from which water is released for re-circulation or the pool completely emptied, certain other fittings are built into the pool when it is initially constructed. The inlet spreader, normally at the shallow end of the pool, is the connection through which recirculated water returns to the pool. There are three basic types – fixed flow, variable flow and variable direction – but they come in numerous forms to suit all types of pools and applications. In certain cases they are placed in the floor of the pool, and specific variations are also available for hydrotherapy use (where the incoming water is utilized for therapeutic massage).

A third integral fixture is a surface skimmer (more usual than a detached skimmer) which, as its name suggests, removes surface debris before it can sink to the pool floor. This is installed below the coping stone, just submerged. Most work off the suction side of the filter pump, though some are gravity controlled on a weir action principle, using a buoyant flap or ring over which the water flows to produce a positive movement at surface level. There are various refinements incorporated into skimmers, such as a linkage with the sump outlet suction line, so that flow

High glass doors lead from the living-room of this house in Washington to the terrace pool spanning the entire width of the garden

can be balanced between skimmer and main drain during filtration, or an equalizer valve which allows water to enter the skimmer from an abnormally low point, should the water level drop unexpectedly, or the skimmer take in air for some other reason. The bigger the pool, the more skimmer units will be needed. As a general guide, one skimmer will service 500 sq ft of water surface, with a maximum flow rate of 2,000 gallons per hour through a fixed skimmer, and 1,000 gallons per hour through a detachable unit.

The other fitting which is usually built into the pool is the vacuum cleaner outlet and plug, although sometimes the vacuum may be operated off the surface skimmer. The outlet always has to be below water level, to prevent air entering the system. If installed midway along one pool side, within reach from the pool edge, the length of hose needed is minimized.

A further fitting, underwater lighting, is best installed at the outset. Lights are normally supplied with a wall niche to house the light fitting from which a sheathed cable is connected to a junction box at deck level. A flexible length of cable will allow the light to be brought to deck level when the bulb needs changing. Most lights operate on a 12 volt supply, and come with the necessary transformer. One light of 250 watts is adequate for a rectangular pool of 500 sq ft surface area, but more may be necessary to accommodate unusual shapes.

For clarity's sake, the mechanical apparatus necessary for pool maintenance is here divided into internal and external fittings. So far only the 'internal' fittings have been discussed.

In the recirculation process, once the water leaves the pool through the sump outlet, it is pumped to the filter tanks, cleaned, sterilized, heated if a heater is installed, and returned to the pool via the inlet spreader. The sequence and fitments involved are highly complex, and it is here that pool owners will expend most time, and might encounter most trouble. The pipe runs which connect the pool to the external equipment are permanently buried underground, usually at a depth of 18 ins. in sand and ideally contained in ducts. Rigid plastic or low density polythene pipes $1\frac{1}{2}$ and 2 in are most durable, and are unlikely to burst under freezing conditions. Rigid plastic is jointed with plastic, polythene with compression fittings.

For domestic pool application two types of pump are used, the self-priming, and non-self priming, and the type you have will largely depend on its location and the location of the filter, as well as the arrangement of pipes. The main difference between them is that a self-priming pump is capable of air extraction from the suction side, which means that it will operate efficiently either above or below water level. Without the addition of a preceding priming tank, a non-self-priming pump cannot extract air from the suction side, and will not pump water efficiently if any air is present. Thus it must usually be placed below water level. As the surface skimmer and vacuum, as well as the sump, are connected to the pump it must be protected from excessive debris by a coarse strainer box, which if not an integral part of the pump unit, must be added. It is important that the flow rate allowed by the pump is matched to the size of the filter tank; too small a tank will inevitably give a short filter cycle, and an oversized pump could also result in the same inefficiency.

The pump recirculates water through the filter apparatus by one of three principles; by pressure by vacuum, or by gravity flow. Pressure or

vacuum filters are the most commonly used, and they can be either the diatomaceous earth type or the permanent media type. Cartridge filters, less costly, are suitable for some small pools, and as well as some sand or gravel filters, utilize the gravity flow principle. The main function of the filter is to clean the water before it is sterilized and recirculated, and consequently the filter itself must from time to time be cleaned. Some are self-cleaning, through the use of a backwash cycle, others can be manually cleaned, whilst others employ various refinements of these principles.

Although it is obvious that the total volume of water in the pool is not filtered in one complete turnover – as cleaned water re-enters the pool, it mixes with dirty water, so the process is rather one of continuous dilution – the filter should be of sufficient rating in gallons per hour to turn over the pool's capacity in eight hours. Thus a pool of 8,000 gallons requires a filter rated at 1,000 gallons per hour. Rate of turnover will possibly vary with the 'bathing load', but this eight hour cycle will suit most domestic pools, as it also allows the filter to work overnight, so that the pool is ready for use each morning, and takes advantage of low cost heating arrangements.

Diatomaceous earth filters clean the water by passing it through a layer of diatomaceous earth, which is a fine white powder composed of diatoms, microscopic marine or vegetable organisms in fossilized skeleton form. Each diatom, invisible to the naked eye, is a porous framework of irregular shape and size. Diatomaceous earth is mined and fairly rare.

In application, the earth is mixed with water to a 'slurry' and fed into the suction side of the pump, through the skimmer, or through a specially designed 'precoat' pot. As the water is pumped through the filter, the earth is retained by screens or septum, and forms a porous layer known as the 'precoat'. Each time the filter is cleaned (usually at three- or four-weekly intervals) the diatomaceous earth must be replaced.

The permanent media filter most common in domestic pools uses sand, sometimes gravel or a substitute, as the 'permanent media' called 'permanent' even though it might need to be replaced after a few years. This filter is a larger unit than the diatomaceous earth filter, and although it

In this spectacular position over-hanging a valley in California, pool and terrace are designed in conjuction with the house. The wide eaves give shade and definition to the terrace and an open verandah runs parallel to the pool. The edges and corners of the pool are gently rounded

Pool and surrounding terrace are built between the house and a large lake; climbing plants cover the concrete aggregate retaining walls. The spring diving board has a sculptured quality. Design by Edward D Dart

costs less to install, is generally more expensive to run. High-rate rapid sand filters, comprised of a special sand bed supported by shingle, do not need precoating, although where certain water conditions exist, a coagulent (alum) is added to the water and pumped through the system to cause flocculation. This provides a gelatinous coating on the sand bed which assists in trapping fine dirt particles which are otherwise difficult to remove. These filters need to be backwashed or otherwise cleaned once a week.

Cartridge filters are available in a wide variety, in all of which a porous filter element is contained wholly within the cartridge. When the filter becomes clogged, the whole filter is generally replaced. As it is suitable only for small scale use, it has not gained widespread usage.

Chlorine, the substance normally used to sterilize domestic swimming pools, can either be added manually, or by a mechanical dosing device. Where the latter is used, it will be attached to the filter, so that filtered water is chlorinated before being returned to the pool. There are several forms of chlorine available for pool use. The most basic, chlorine gas, is normally used only for larger public pools, but where it is in domestic use, must be carefully applied and stored according to safety regulations. Your contractor will be aware of these standards, and will certainly see that they are employed. Sodium hypochlorite, generally called liquid chlorine, is more often used domestically, or sometimes calcium hypochlorite, which comes in tablet or granular form. Both are likely to cause excess alkalinity in the water, disturbing the pH, or balance between acid and alkaline substances, and this must be counteracted by the addition of acid. The test kit supplied by most contractors, as well as indicating whether the correct amount of chlorine is being used, will also determine the pH of the water.

A third and most recently developed form of chlorine for pool use is cyanurate, which has the advantage of not being dissipated by sunlight, as are other forms of chlorine. Where it is used, the pool should first be preconditioned with a dose of cyanuric acid.

Most domestic pools employ the marginal method of chlorine application, which means that the low chlorine content of the water will occasionally need to be boosted by an extra strong dose, probably once a month, or whenever there are apparent signs of algae developing.

As well as chlorination and pH, which should be maintained slightly alkaline at 7.2 to 7.4, treatment of pool water also involves special additives for algae control. Algae, tiny water plants, cause discolouration of the water, foster bacteria growth, and can clog filters, form slime, and decrease the effectiveness of chlorine as a sterilizing agent. Special algicides are available to assist in control of algae, and as they are more stable chemically than chlorine, they remain in the water much longer. They are added to the pool in a specified dose, which will be directed by the manufacturer.

If the pool is to be heated, this will normally take place after the water has been filtered and sterilized, and before it is recirculated to the pool. The same pump which forces the water through the filter is normally used to continue the movement of water through the heating apparatus.

Water for pool use in Northern climates can be most effectively heated by electricity, by gas or oil fired burner. The advantages of an electrical system are that the unit itself is compact and not expensive to install, unless long cable runs are involved, and running costs can be reduced by using an 'off-peak' service, eminently suited for this application because it means the pool can be heated overnight, ready for use the next day. Before deciding on electricity, however, it is wise to find out whether your local electricity authority can accept the loading on the existing supply.

When a gas or oil fired burner is used, it can be either the one existing for ordinary household use, or a separate installation. In the former instance, a special heat exchanger or calorifier must be introduced, permitting the flow of hot water from the boiler to be piped through the main flow of pool water. Water for pool use must be controlled by a separate thermostat to the domestic supply, and this, coupled with other special requirements, sometimes makes this an uneconomical method to employ. When a separate boiler is introduced for pool use, although its running costs are comparatively low, this might be offset by installation costs, especially if a by-pass or exchanger is necessary to eliminate the flow of cold water through the boiler. This, in turn, produces condensation that might corrode the lining.

Sometimes a multi-jet town or bottled gas unit, similar to those for domestic use, is a convenient method, because water is taken straight through the heater, with perhaps the addition of a simple by-pass to take some of the flow; this, however, this makes a comparatively expensive fuel.

In general, the type of heating you choose will be dictated by the maximum temperature you require (72° F is considered appropriate for a normal domestic pool); the months of the year in which the pool needs heating; the location; heating speed required; whether the pool is enclosed/covered/indoors; and the ratio of pool surface area to total gallonage. Presuming that it will be necessary to heat the pool for at least five months of the year, the average 12,000 gallon pool consumes about 450 therms over that period, increasing up to 700 if the pool is uncovered.

Building and landscaping a terrace

With modern materials and methods, there is a terrace to be had for any purpose in any climate, from the smallest apartment to the largest house. By strict definition, a terrace is a raised, level place for walking, with vertical or sloping fronts or sides, faced with a retaining material. However, the word is used here to encompass any man-made addition or extension.

As well as personal preference, choice of a terrace design is largely a matter of requirements, available space, existing architecture, and economy. In general, the requirements of a terrace are that it should be a place to enjoy a garden or outdoor atmosphere while still retaining some of the refinements of indoor living. Thus it must provide suitable space for benches, chairs and tables, and perhaps outdoor cooking facilities, for any number of people from half a dozen to twenty. It should be appropriately sheltered from wind and excessive sun, so that its use is not restricted to perfect weather, rare in any climate, and should be sufficiently well lit to accommodate night-time activity. It must be attractive, comfortable and practical.

As for available space – owners of a pocket-handkerchief garden can, with a little ingenious planning, create a terrace as attractive as any on a large scale.

Whether a terrace design takes its measure from existing architecture or not is a matter of how close the affiliation is to be. Obviously, any separate entity may legitimately be allowed to develop a character of its own, or to take on the guise of the garden which surrounds it. But if the terrace extends from a house or pool, take care to blend with discretion – proportion, materials, and atmosphere. Fortunately, a terrace is one home improvement which can be undertaken by the most un-handy home handyman, and still be guaranteed a reasonable measure of success. If the design itself is simple, and there are no siting difficulties, the cost of materials need not be great, and the whole thing can be accomplished most economically. Elaborations can then be made by stages. Even if cost is no object, it is always wise to leave scope for additions and changes.

Whichever basic form your terrace is to take, there are certain design generalizations which apply equally to each, if the terrace is to blend successfully with its surrounds. Because it will be part of a whole, there must be a careful consideration of height, breadth, shape and colour if the balance of all these elements is to be maintained. In practice, this means that simply defining boundaries, and the arbitrary allocation of dimensions, is not enough. Ground area and height must be weighed against the visible ground area and height of the structure to which the terrace is attached, or to the mass and layout of the surrounding garden. These factors should be considered from several physical angles; inside looking out, from middle and far distance looking in, and from approaches, especially if the terrace is set amidst a garden.

A flagstoned terrace enclosed by the house and accessible through the covered entrance and tall sliding windows. The corners of the terrace, left unpaved, have been planted with shrubs and evergreens that will provide colour in winter, whilst pots of geraniums are introduced during the summer months

Small sheltered terrace protected by the house and a high screening glazed wall. On either side, at a lower level, are flower beds planted with ferns and young trees. A small bridge crosses the gap between indoor and outdoor sitting areas

Climate, too, has its effect on terrace design. Where strong prevailing winds and extensive sunshine make shelter and shade a necessity, walls and coverings should be considered integral design features, rather than additions. A site on the south side of the house will usually provide a reasonable amount of shelter. A little to the east the terrace will catch the sun earlier in the day, and the glare of evening sun will be cut off by the corner of the house. And a little to the west, the house will afford the terrace shelter from easterly winds, and paving will hold the warmth of the sun for longer. Where side walls are used for additional protection, i.e. on the east and west sides of a terrace facing north, a solid structure will provide calm conditions in its lee for a length of up to three times its height. Beyond this, the lee is subject to downdraughts. Hedges or slatted screens filter the wind, materially reducing its speed and strength for up to six times the wall's height.

Even if your terrace is adequately sheltered without the addition of walls, these may be necessary for another reason. Where the land drops away at the edge of a terrace, it may create an uncomfortable, insecure feeling, which is most easily eliminated by the addition of a visual barrier of some kind at the terrace edge. If a wall is not practical, then a low balustrade or hedge, or even a bank of plant boxes, will usually serve the purpose. In the reverse situation, where the land rises at the edge of the terrace, it should be remembered that the rise is best left clear of walls or dense foliage which can give the terrace below a claustrophobic atmosphere. Far better to taper plantings away from the rise, low in the front and taller in the distance. Terrace approaches play an important part in the successful end result, and must therefore be considered together with the actual terrace design. Paths should be proportionate in width, and should be built of like or complementary materials. If the terrace is formal, its approaches, too, should be reasonably ordered in feeling. Once you have decided on the form, location and design of the terrace, the next step is to choose the materials of which it is to be constructed. The choice is usually between paving of some kind, laid over an appropriate surface, and timber, for verandahs and decks, and sometimes balconies. These

latter three, together with the lanai and sun roof, are structural additions, and must be considered by an architect or structural engineer, which thus puts them outside the scope of this book.

All paving for outdoor use should be durable, and sufficiently textured to provide a safe footing when wet. Timber should always be hardwood, oiled, and treated with a moisture-proof coating. The materials most commonly used for paving are concrete, brick, stone, artificial stone, earthenware or marble, ceramic tiles and hardwood blocks.

Concrete can be poured in situ, to form one continuous surface, and finished with a simple cement render, or suitable paving paint. This method, however, is rather inflexible, and does not make the best use of plants, shrubs, and the softer elements of terrace design. Far more suitable are the large concrete slabs available from stonemasons and garden suppliers. Granite concrete slabs are less likely to scale or crack than gravel concrete, and should be used in preference whenever possible.

If you use brick, choose a hard, well-burnt type. If it happens to be available, reclaimed brick is economical, and its time-mellowed colourings invariably blend more easily with an established setting. Bricks lend themselves to a fascinating variety of paving patterns. They can be used broad side up, or laid on their narrow edge, or in a combination of the two. The hardest part is calculating the number of bricks you need; as a guideline, remember that an 8 ft by 20 ft area requires three hundred standard bricks laid broad side up, and four hundred and fifty laid narrow side up.

Stone for paving purposes comes in many types, and your choice will largely depend on availability; it is obviously more economical to use a local stone, and also more aesthetically correct, since the stone will look at its best in its natural environment. 'Soft' stones, such as limestone and sandstone, weather rapidly, and also need special cutting and forming. Their softness and geological structure makes them eminently suited to cutting in irregular shapes, and laying in a random pattern—the so-called crazy paving, which, although not held in the same favour as it once was, still makes an attractive surface in an informal setting. 'Hard' stones, such

Wedge-shaped pool with non-slip stepping stones of concrete aggregate across the narrow end. The terrace has a dining table and is equipped with downlighters for late evenings and blinds to shield the area from strong sunlight

as granite, usually come in square or rectangular blocks, because their extreme hardness makes irregular shaping almost an impossibility. Granite can sometimes be reclaimed from old buildings. One of the most economical forms of paving for outdoor use (and extremely practical, too, since it was specifically designed for the purpose), is the artificial stone slab.

Although river-washed or bluestone gravels make a relatively inexpensive surfacing, they have certain practical disadvantages for overall use. Gravel is not particularly safe to walk on, since it is unstable and slippery, especially when wet. Since it is a loose surfacing it is invariably tramped inside the house, or inadvertently swept away from the terrace surface, and must be continually replaced. In addition, it is hard to keep a loose gravel surface free of unwanted weeds and grass, and it requires constant clearing and raking if it is to remain tidy. If you do want to use gravel on your terrace, however, there are two solutions to the problems it presents: one, to embed the gravel in concrete or cement; and two, to use it in combination with stable paving, and confine the gravel to small, secondary areas. Thus used, it is shown to best advantage.

Hardwood blocks, though perhaps not as durable as concrete and stone surfacings, induce a pleasant rustic atmosphere, especially if they are combined with wooden garden furniture and casual plantings. Such slabs come in squares or rectangles, or in circles when they have been hewn straight off the tree trunk. The type of timber used depends again on what is locally available; but by choice, a broad-grained variety weathers best.

Tiles and marble are, obviously, the aristocrats of paving materials, and using them over a large area is expensive. Earthenware and terra-cotta tiles, or 'quarry' tiles as they are often called, are less costly than the special ceramic tiles made for outdoor use, but do not have the same colour range. Marble comes in a number of colours, pinks greens and blacks being more expensive; it must always be cut and laid by a stone mason.

The method of laying paving in most circumstances is not difficult, and can be done by the layman with a limited budget but time and energy to spare. The first step, after marking out the area, is to excavate to a depth of approximately 9 ins, then level the ground by raking and tamping. Refill with a layer of rubble, then coarse sand, or for greater strength, poured concrete. Allowing approximately $\frac{1}{2}$ in between each of the paving blocks – and remembering to leave unpaved pockets for plants – simply lay them in the required pattern on the sand (or bed in the wet concrete), and tap down firmly with a hammer handle, checking the level as you go. The joints between the stones can be grouted with a strong, slightly moistened mixture of two parts sand to one part cement, and pressed down firmly with a piece of three-ply to ensure that joints are tight and well-packed. If pointed to within $\frac{1}{4}$ in of the paving's surface, this allows sufficient space for moss to eventually form, and give the paving a finished, natural look. Alternatively, the joints between stones can be filled with earth and planted; low-growing varieties which will not be affected when trodden are best, and particularly suited are herbs and others which give off a pleasant fragrance when crushed underfoot. The terrace should be finished at the perimeters with a fillet of mortar to hold the sand foundation intact, or preferably with a low wall.

Draining the terrace properly is particularly important for its long-term efficient operation. Always slope the surface towards the perimeters –

Opposite Tall sliding doors make the terrace an extension of the living-room in this Danish house; downlighters are fixed in the over-hanging roof

Below Paving in radiating petals makes a lively pattern for this terrace in France

approximately 2 ins in 10 ft is sufficient – and install corner drains so that run off is directed away from the site, and not left to accumulate and rot foundations. If timber decking is used, the covered area should be well ventilated, and there should be no opportunity for debris, such as dead leaves, to gather under the wood, where they will cause decay.

The requirements of the sun roof, are, of course, different to those of a ground-level terrace. Weight, drainage and wind are the most important considerations. The added weight of plant containers, soil, furniture – and people – must not be too much for foundations, roofing joists and supporting walls to bear in safety, and it may be necessary to consult an engineer to ensure that the ratio is right. As a general rule, a flat roof surface will bear a weight of four hundred pounds to one square yard. Screens will invariably be necessary on a sun roof, either to shield a disagreeable view, or as wind breaks (the wind velocity is greater at roof height than on the ground). Lightweight materials should be used in preference to concrete or bricks, and where possible, supporting posts should be screwed or bolted to existing walls. Otherwise lateral supports can be used, disguised with vines and plants if they are unsightly. Also for reasons of the weight it adds, paving is not advisable on a sun roof. Suitable substitutes are mineral-finished roofing felt, exterior quality vinyl sheeting or asbestos tiles.

Walls and railings

There are two distinct reasons for incorporating a wall or railing in a terrace; in the first instance, to screen against wind or an unwanted view, or to create a specified optical effect; and in the second, as a safety measure, e.g. as a wall or rail for enclosing a swimming pool. Walls can be

The paved terrace of this German house is partially covered by the overhanging upper storey. A convenient design which provides a shaded or dry dining area, play space for the children, or store for garden furniture. Design by Wilhelm Haug

solid, in brick, concrete, stone or timber, or the 'filter' type, in lattice, wattle, or openwork pattern of hard material; railings will be either pre-fabricated in metal, or purpose-made in timber. As well as suitability for purpose, walls and railings should be chosen to reflect the architectural character of any structure to which they are attached.

Any solid retaining wall more than 4 ft high is a major construction work, and should be left to a competent bricklayer. For those who wish to undertake the task themselves, the pre-fabricated, interlocking concrete blocks made specifically for the purpose, and which come with full instructions from the manufacturer are very easy to work with. For the more adventurous, the following guidelines will be a starting point.

Dry stone walls should rest on good foundations. Excavate the site to a depth of approximately 9 ins, and pack with rubble to a depth of 6 ins, then cover with 2–3 ins of concrete bedding. If the wall is a retaining wall (as opposed to a free-standing wall), clear the space so that work can be done from both sides; the soil can then be placed in final position after the wall is completed. Lay the first course of stone in the wet concrete, bedding carefully and leaving until the concrete has set. Build gradually on this base, using sifted soil to a $\frac{1}{2}$-in depth to bed the stones as you go. As the wall rises, it should have a slight lean towards the soil side, and be interspersed at 6 ft intervals with a long anchor stone reaching out into the retaining soil. A free-standing wall uses similar building techniques, but because it lacks the support of soil on one side, must have a firm base and taper inwards on both sides, so that the base is the widest part.

Artificial stones and brick are easier to use than random walling stones, because of their regular shape, but they must be mortar jointed, and thus do not provide the same opportunity for plantings in the wall as do dry methods. All solid walls should be securely topped with coping stones bedded in mortar, or with a layer of plain concrete to prevent stones from falling, and to keep rain and frost from weakening the interior.

There are many ways to use timber for walls, both of the solid and filter type, and generally, the more complex the design and method, the more expensive the wall. One of the most attractive patterns developed in latter years is the 'board on board' method, where 4 in boards are placed at 6-in intervals on both sides of the wall, so that boards and spaces overlap. This construction can be either horizontal or vertical; used vertically, the view from the terrace is not entirely obstructed. Since most timber fencing is made from soft wood, it should be treated with an exterior grade preservative to extend its life.

Apart from pre-fabricated trellis and lattice, so well suited to vines and climbers, a filter screen can also be most attractive in wattle, usually available in pre-fabricated lengths from nurseries. Hedges, too, can be used in this way, although they do carry with them the permanent incon-venience of having to be regularly clipped into shape.

Unless they are to be purpose-made in timber, most railings are pre-fabricated in rust-proof metal, and should be embedded in concrete. The metal railing looks best when it is finished with a coating of exterior quality paint, which also affords a certain amount of protection against rust. Pre-fabricated masonry railings are also available, but these usually tend towards the low balustrade type, and are decorative rather than practical in application.

A miscellany of paving with concrete slabs, large flat stones and mosaic

Overhead coverings

It somehow seems like a contradiction in terms to refer to a terrace as having a roof, but frequently it is desirable to add a lightweight overhead covering, not only for comfort, but also for practical reasons if the terrace has a service as well as recreational function. Such a 'roof' can be a permanently fixed translucent sheeting, in glass fibre or plastic, a pergola, or an awning.

Pergolas are shade-makers rather than anything else, as the network of vines which covers them is not exactly rainproof. They are usually made of timber, though bamboo and metal can be used, on a slat and beam construction supported by pillars embedded in the terrace paving. Unfortunately, most of the favourite climbers for pergolas – wistaria, grape and so forth – are also deciduous, which means a leaf-gathering problem. It is wise to also include an evergreen vine, so that the pergola is cloaked in more than a straggle of bare trailers in winter.

Awnings come in canvas, plastic or glass fibre fabrics, and can be fixed or retractable. An 8-ft awning will be sufficiently supported by hinged and folding brackets, whereas a 12-ft width will need the additional support of fixed or semi-permanent (i.e. slotted into prepared grooves or holes, and seasonally removed) poles at the outer edges. Be sure that a fixed awning is taut enough, and sufficiently sloped, to permit rainwater to run off; even the most resistant fabric, will, in time, be adversely affected by permanent puddles. Take care also with your colour choice; too many, or too strong a mixture will kill the subtleties of flower colours and dominate the terrace to the detriment of every other feature. The same rule applies to garden umbrellas, which are more convenient and less costly shade-makers than awnings in climates where the sun is unlikely to cause major discomfort.

Apart from man-made structures, trees, hedges and shrubs will provide shelter and shade on a terrace, if planted with regard to prevailing winds and aspect. They are not advisable on and around pool terraces, however, as the accumulated debris eventually spreads to the pool water. Trees to use are evergreens with dense foliage, not so tall or fast growing as to cut off light and sunshine altogether. And they should never be planted where roots will spread and eventually crack foundations. If it is possible, visit a nursery, aboretum or the local botanical gardens before you select trees and shrubs, so that you can ascertain exactly their potential dimensions and density.

Ornamentation

In talking about statues for use in gardens, it is as well to rid oneself of the conventional image. Certainly a Rodin is a handsome addition, and certainly a piece of statuary may be an Adonis or a Pan, a dove or a frog sculpted in stone or moulded in concrete, but in current terms, it can just as well be a fountain, a piece of driftwood or weathered sandstone, or simply two rocks in a gravel bed, Japanese fashion. In other words, anything which is beautiful to the eye of the beholder can stand unadorned on a terrace in the name of statuary, and should, since a terrace has the same right to be personalized as any other part of your house. If there is any 'rule' about the use of such ornamentation, perhaps it is that it must

Well-placed spotlights create night-time reflections in this small oval pool within a paved terrace

A small brick terrace built in the sheltered corner between house and boundary wall. Collapsible campaign chairs and slatted wooden table are overhung by the wooden-boarded split

Right Roof-top pool and terrace overlooking the trees of Neuilly. Around the edge the raised border of shrubs links roof with tree tops. Comfortable wooden chairs have raked backs, and the awnings of the pool house and umbrella provide shade. Designed by architect Leopold Vitorage and landscaped by Maurice-Jean Vidal

harmonize with its surroundings; a modern sculpture can be used in a formal, traditional setting as long as both have simplicity as their keynote.

Urns, tubs, plant containers, statues, fountains–and of course plants– all make their contribution to terrace decoration, and it is the pieces you choose as well as the way they are combined which will finally characterize the terrace.

Urns, in the traditional sense, can be used in much the same way as statues – standing simply to be admired – if their symmetry and grace warrant it. Most available from conventional sources, however, need the addition of plants if they are to pay their way as a design element.

Formal or random, classic or modern, there are plant containers made to suit all moods. And apart from this enormous variety of commercially available containers, one's own ingenuity and imagination can add indefinitely to the list; old fire grates, stone horse troughs, brass spittoons —anything which looks attractive and holds soil can be used as a plant container. Concrete and cement containers come in all shapes, sizes and colours, but their weight tends to mean that once installed, they are not easily moved – important to remember if you are relying on change-abouts to keep up a continual showing of colour all through the year. For trailing plants, special tiered earthenware pots are most attractive, or if you can find one, a barrel from which circular plugs can be removed in the sides. Halved barrels are also useful containers for ornamental trees and larger shrubs. In recent years, fibreglass containers have come into extensive use. They are light, very durable, and can be obtained as facsimiles of classic shapes, appropriately coloured, or in clean, crisp modern shapes to complement modern outdoor furniture. In planning the distribution of containers, bear in mind that those of less than 6 ins diameter look lost, even on a small terrace, and should be grouped in threes and fours. Proportion plays an important part in design, and one of the most attractive ways to add height is with hanging baskets. These can be staged at different levels and filled with trailing plants, and effectively take care of any discrepancy between width and height. Alternatively, a tiered arrangement of wall-supported troughs, a vertical garden if you like, can have the same effect, and is particularly useful on small terraces where surface space may be required for furniture.

Lighting

A terrace should be lit for practical reasons, but also to increase its optical dimension. If the terrace is close to a domestic power source, so much the better, for it is a simple matter to extend electric leads and conceal them beneath foliage. Where this is not possible, electric power can be supplied from a portable generator, or bottled gas used to light flares and lamps. Lighting should be subtle and looks well concealed behind foliage along the terrace perimeter. If a keener light is required for eating or other activities, use candles or candle lamps at the source. Pools and special ornamental features should be spot lit, as should the garden beyond the terrace – there is nothing quite so alluring and mysterious as a garden which seems to extend into the night, which will be the effect that is achieved if certain central features are pinpointed by light, and less important features left to fade into shadow.

Spectacular pool tucked into the
hillside terrace of Norman Parkinson's
house overlooking a bay in Tobago.
A profusion of flowers including
bougainvillea, zinnias, petunias and
geraniums, line both pool and terrace

Two views of a pool designed for a
weekend house. The living-room opens
directly onto the pool decking with
full-height glazed sliding doors. Lights
in the extended ceiling illuminate the
terrace. There are plastic covered
cushions to sit on scattered casually
on the terrace at the water's edge.
Design by Marcel Bretos
and David Napoli

Left The perfect terrace for dining out of doors in summer months is found in this old barn. The wall towards the garden was demolished and the floor bricked in a chequered pattern

Above Extravagant use of climbing ivy and amelopsis shades and decorates this paved terrace which provides an attractive extension from the main living room

Above A tiny casual terrace set
beneath the high ivy-covered wall of
a garden. The area is paved with the
cross cuts of a tree trunk which makes
a pattern of disks. It is bounded by
rough stones, with a barbecue set in

Right A courtyard terrace in cool
grey-blue and white. The ornamental
ironwork is set off by the plain
flowerpots, chequered tiles and simple
whitewashed walls. Design
by John Brookes

Above Green and white theme for a modern atrium, with a partly slatted glassed roof to shield sun-seekers from breezes while they stretch out on full length chairs

Right A terrace in Milan, shaded by vines massed on a timber pergola. Against the warm brick tones, white 'campaign' chairs make a pleasing contrast

Opposite A stunning rooftop terrace with slatted wooden sun shield overhead. Shrubs in waist-high white cement boxes enclose the terrace, blotting out surrounding roof tops. Design by Aldo Jacobs

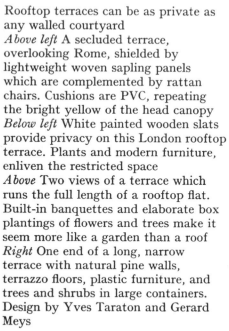

Rooftop terraces can be as private as any walled courtyard

Above left A secluded terrace, overlooking Rome, shielded by lightweight woven sapling panels which are complemented by rattan chairs. Cushions are PVC, repeating the bright yellow of the head canopy

Below left White painted wooden slats provide privacy on this London rooftop terrace. Plants and modern furniture, enliven the restricted space

Above Two views of a terrace which runs the full length of a rooftop flat. Built-in banquettes and elaborate box plantings of flowers and trees make it seem more like a garden than a roof

Right One end of a long, narrow terrace with natural pine walls, terrazzo floors, plastic furniture, and trees and shrubs in large containers. Design by Yves Taraton and Gerard Meys

Above left North African influence in this walled suntrap shows clearly in the low level built-in seating, splashed with colour to highlight the all-white surrounds
Below left A white-fringed Brazilian hammock and white floor cushions are used for lounging on an open terrace. Design by Salier, Courtois and Lajus
Above right Rooftop terrace with a sparkling, all white dining area, set against a lush screen of plants. Design by Albini
Opposite Superbly architectural roof terrace with concrete rafters and geometric paving of white marble, contrasted with the wavy lines of moulded fibreglass furniture

Pool houses and pool enclosures

Apart from the building which contains pool plant and equipment, most private swimming pools incorporate some form of changing room at the poolside. No matter how close the main house bathroom and dressing facilities may be, it is invariably more convenient for the pool to have its own, if only to save the house from the scourge of wet footprints and dripping bodies. These can be as simple or as elaborate as you like, depending on how much the pool will be used as an all-round recreational facility, and how much you are willing to spend on pool improvements. It is really rather pointless to build a pool house without installing a shower and WC, so you must expect your outlay to cover these costs. The simplest, and most inexpensive form is a pre-fabricated shed in aluminium or fibreglass, which offers a certain intrinsic degree of insulation, and can be erected in a short time without professional assistance. By keeping the pool house as close as possible to existing services – and this applies to the most basic and the most elaborate structures – plumbing costs will be kept to a minimum; and in any case, the shorter the pipe runs, the less the chance of plumbing problems developing.

If you go to the expense of having a pool house custom designed and built, presumably you will want it to contain more elaborate fittings and equipment – a properly fitted bathroom with at least two shower cubicles, a couple of changing rooms, and perhaps an indoor sitting/dining room for use in extremely hot weather. It is increasingly usual to find pool houses fitted with saunas, and considering a perfectly adequate sauna bath can be installed for a couple of hundred pounds, they are well worth the investment for their health benefits. There is no better way to rid oneself of city grime and tension than to laze away twenty minutes in that warm, humid atmosphere, as Scandinavians and other devotees have known for a hundred years and more. Although traditionally heated by natural means, most saunas these days are electrically heated, and usually of the 'dry' heat variety. Their construction is highly skilled, and they must be installed by one of the companies who specialize in this; your pool contractor should be able to direct you to a reputable manufacturer.

Another sophistication frequently found in conjunction with a sauna is a solarium, an artificial sun lamp. As opposed to a portable sun lamp, a solarium is a much more elaborate affair, which must be installed by the manufacturer and fixed in position. They are obtainable at a starting price of around a hundred pounds or so. It is possible to extend the list of health equipment for the pool side use almost ad infinitum – exercise equipment, electrically operated massage and vibrator machines, hydrotherapy apparatus, including electronic impulse showers, are just a few of the more common – and the only real limitations are those of cost, and

Opposite Cane hanging chair and irregularly laid bricks add an air of informality to this well-planned terrace, where barbecue and bench seating are incorporated in the design of the house

A Gothick pavilion is at the semi-circular end of the pool with shallow steps leading into the water. Wooden boxes with agapanthus stand along the edge. Design by Godfrey Allen

how many hours a day you can put aside to use these facilities.

It should be noted here that if the pool house is to be used in a wider recreational sense, then provision should be made at the outset for additional facilities, including indoor games and perhaps even guest bedrooms. In addition, there may be a need for heating, so that the pool and its facilities can be enjoyed year-round; and to reap the maximum benefits from your investment, the pool house needs to be planned and decorated with the same degree of care as you would extend to any room in your house. Heating a pool house is much the same as heating any other house, and the method you use will depend on existing services; but for economy reasons, it is as well to consider this in conjunction with the type of heating used for the pool, as one plant to the normal domestic supply may serve both. Decorative ideas for pool houses will be more fully discussed in the following chapters; here, it is sufficient to say that all interior finishes, fittings and furniture should be in materials which are not affected by moisture – aluminium hardware, PVC, acrylic and plastic furniture and fabrics, hard surface floor coverings – so that maintenance costs and effort will be kept to a minimum.

Pool covers

A pool cover for an outdoor swimming pool can be a desirable piece of ancillary equipment for any number of reasons. It can be a safety measure; a means of reducing the intake of surface debris; an insulator to reduce overnight water heat loss if the pool is heated; or a winter cover for the pool, to prevent frost and ice cracking its surface. There are many types available, and much experimentation is currently in progress to find the perfect pool cover, which, as manufacturers readily admit, has not yet been invented. In the meantime, those in most popular use are as follows, and their manufacturers will be known to your pool contractor.

The suspended woven or continuous plastic film cover is anchored by special fastenings to the paving around the pool, or held down at the edges by a water tube or special ballast tubes; some of these simply settle on the water surface, while more recent versions are slightly inflated to a dome shape, so that surface rain water can run off on to the pool surrounds. The standard insulating cover, usually designed to float on the water surface, is used in one piece for smaller pools, but for anything over 24 ft by 12 ft in

Simple modern bathing pavilion is made of cedar with a glass-fibre cover. The area is paved and there are two interlocking changing rooms and a long bench that can be used for storage. Design by Timothy Rendle

dimension, is fitted with a roller mechanism or used in sections. If you are prepared for the expense of it, you can have a rigid, mechanized cover custom made, but considering that a full-scale pool enclosure is not appreciably more expensive, such a cover is rarely warranted. The fourth type of pool cover, a safety and maintenance measure rather than for insulation, is made of fine mesh netting in a weather-proof fibre, and firmly anchored to the pool edges. Finally, it is worth mentioning here something which is more a device for pool metamorphosis than a cover, and very definitely a luxury item. This is the hydraulically controlled floor which, at the flick of a switch, slides out to cover the water surface completely, transforming a pool into an instant dance and party place. It is designed for use on both indoor and outdoor pools, and must, of course, be carefully engineered by professionals. Costly, but judging by its success so far, an idea worth consideration if you wish to expand the scope of your pool complex to the optimum.

Pool enclosures

Except for tropical climates, there are few places in the world where a pool will not benefit from the addition of an enclosure. This offers the same advantage as an indoor pool – year-round, comfortable swimming conditions – and if the enclosure is a portable one, contains the added bonus of reverting to an outdoor pool during the summer months. There is a type of enclosure to suit every requirement, and the choice will largely be determined by economic, climatic and space considerations. In accounting for space, bear in mind that any pool enclosure should allow a minimum surround between pool edge and enclosure of 2 ft on three sides, and 4 ft on the entrance side.

Traditional or 'heavy' enclosures are the most expensive type, and require the services of an architect. They are constructed of brick, stone, concrete or timber – virtually turning an outdoor pool into a separately located indoor pool – and have as their principal advantage a high degree of natural insulation, which reduces internal heating costs. This is especially the case if translucent panels are incorporated in the building so that maximum use is made of solar heat gain. Such enclosures should be mechanically heated and ventilated to eliminate condensation problems, and insulated to reduce the noise factor, just as is the case with indoor swimming pools.

Medium to lightweight enclosures are generally available in pre-fabricated form, framed in aluminium or lightweight treated steel, timber laminates or pre-cast concrete, and using insulated infill panels of glass fibre, Plexiglas or similar translucent or transparent material, and sometimes an opaque surfacing. Their natural insulation properties are reasonably developed, and heating is quickly and economically accomplished. Again, they may make use of solar gain. These enclosures can be regarded as semi-permanent, and some types are provided with all-round sliding doors, so that they may remain in position yet still be opened up in sunny weather. There are two kinds of enclosure which can be classified as lightweight. One is metal or timber framed, using infill panels of Perspex, PVC or Fibreglass. And the second is the inflatable 'air house' type of enclosure. Both these are inexpensive, portable (they can be removed

Opposite Shaded wooded site for a pavilion of classical symmetry complete with Arcadian statues and trellis, making patterns of shade in the interior. A fountain in a shallow pool plays immediately in front, and below is the larger swimming pool. Around the edge irregular paving disappears into the undergrowth

Below Cottage-style pool house made of pine comprises sauna, changing or shower-room and even a living-room

during summer), and have a solar factor almost the equivalent of glass, which may preclude internal heating altogether if the pool water is heated. They do not, however, offer the same visual elegance as a more permanent type of enclosure. Entrance and exit to the former type is generally through sliding doors, and in the case of the latter, by zip fastener or flap, or where traffic is heavy, by a revolving or double door air lock arrangement.

There are three important factors to be considered in the construction of any pool enclosure: heating and ventilation, noise level, and the application of materials used within the structure. Water heating has already been discussed in the second chapter of this book; here, we are concerned only with space heating. Solar heating can be used, where appropriate conditions exist, or the interior of the enclosure can be warmed by a mechanical device. Starting with the most expensive, these are the water-to-air-fanned unit heater of convector; radiators; hot air or hot water pipes; floor or wall embedded element panels; direct or indirect radiant heat; and direct air heaters with fans operated by electricity, gas or oil-fired burners. As well as the type of structure and the volume of air to be heated, choice will depend on existing services, and a decision should be made only after consultation with the enclosure manufacturer and heating experts. Ventilation can be by natural means – which offers little or no control, and is therefore not usually satisfactory – or by mechanical means. Any kind of mechanical ventilator should heat fresh air to room temperature as it enters the enclosure, to avoid discomfort for bathers and extensive misting, and humid air should be extracted at the opposite end of the pool by extractor fans, controlled by humidistats. Since the method of heating employed will largely determine the effectiveness of ventilation, these two factors should be considered in conjunction. In turn, the effectiveness of both these mechanized systems will be affected by bathing

Glass-roofed indoor pool is positioned between two pavilions of a complex house. Flowers and shrubs are planted around the edge of the paved area, which contains tables and chairs for entertaining

load, water temperature and resulting condensation. The human body loses six times as much heat to water as it does to air, yet also needs oxygen to produce its own optimum heat energy. Therefore if the lungs must cope with undue condensation, as well as carbon dioxide and chlorine vapours, all of which reduce the percentage of oxygen in the atmosphere, they will function at a reduced level of efficiency, causing bathers discomfort. Highly technical as it might sound, the importance of suitable heating and ventilation within the enclosure cannot be stressed enough; after all, if its benefits are to be lost by lack of attention to important details, there is hardly any point in having an enclosure at all.

The warmth, light, heat and air of an ideal climate, and conditions which afford the body greatest comfort, either in or out of the water – those are the things which you want from a pool enclosure, and with care they should not be difficult to achieve.

Covered pool with retractable roof is made of anodized aluminium with glass-fibre or glass panels. The enclosed area provides space for sitting out, a play area and room for the pool equipment

Furnishing pool and terrace

Whatever furniture you choose for outdoor use, it must, first of all, be weatherproof; it must also be comfortable enough to accommodate the more relaxed attitudes which go with sitting and lounging in the sun. With the large selection that is available, both in terms of materials and design, it is easy to fulfil these requirements and still achieve a look which complements the basic style of your terrace.

Scale is very important, and space. Because an outdoor area lacks the boundary definition of four solid walls, take special care to note the density of garden areas and other decorative features, and proportion furniture accordingly. As for space, somehow people need more of it in a casual setting. The following points should be considered when arranging your terrace furniture. A bench 6 ft long needs a space 6 ft by 4 ft to seat three people; a space of at least 8 ft by 8 ft is necessary to accommodate a small table and four chairs; and the minimum requirement for two average-length benches, a table and six chairs, allowing for adequate through-traffic flow, is a terrace area 20 ft by 10 ft.

Because it is a natural material, timber is very well suited for use outdoors. Timber furniture can be either rustic in design, suitable for a cottage atmosphere, or of the more formal, modern variety. It is usually only produced in rot-resistant woods, such as teak and Californian redwood, which then simply need a coat of linseed oil to prevent them drying, and to bring up the natural, rich colour – although they can be painted, or stained to any colour with a standard commercial preparation. Modern timber furniture tends to be rather large and solid in design, and is thus most practical equipped with castors. For all furniture for use outside the house, cushions and mattresses should be covered – and filled – with waterproof materials.

Cane and wicker are traditional for outdoor use, and treated with a waterproof coating or painted, will give many years of wear. They can be elaborate or simple in design (remember that elaborate designs have more crevices and corners to catch dust and cobwebs) and their extreme lightness makes them very versatile; not only chairs and tables, but swing seats also are amongst the large range you can expect to find.

There are many types of metal used for outdoor furniture. All-metal seats without upholstery are best avoided, as they can become too hot to sit on when the sun is really out, and those which combine metal and fabric are a more comfortable choice. Wrought iron, cast iron and cast aluminium, steel and aluminium tube frame are the most usual, and the permutations and combinations in which they come are endless. For formal settings, wrought iron is an excellent choice, and looks particularly attractive combined with marble or stone. Wrought iron chairs will always need

This paved roof terrace with direct access to the living-room has a low brick retaining wall. Along one side a wide timber boarded bench supports the portable barbecue

cushions for comfort, and the metal does need constant treatment – paint or other rust-proof coating – to maintain its good looks.

Cast iron furniture has largely been superseded by its modern, lightweight counterpart, cast aluminium. It comes in colours as well as white, and the Chippendale style is amongst its most popular and attractive designs.

Metal frame and tube furniture, as long as the metal is rust-proof, offers a wide and appealing choice, frequently with the bonus of being fold-up, and thus portable for use elsewhere, or winter storage. Amongst the various safari chairs, deck chairs and collapsible chairs which you will find, the special province of metal frame furniture is the reclining easy chair, often part of a suite, which is extremely comfortable and flexible, and well worth consideration. Interesting, too, are the free-standing screens which are sometimes available to match chairs and tables; as well as acting as portable wind-breaks, they make useful changing cubicles. When metal-frame furniture is clad in canvas rather than a waterproof material, it is as well to ensure that the covers will slip off easily so they can be quickly stored in wet weather. Plastic and hemp webbing on metal frames, although inexpensive and quite handsome, does not make the most comfortable of seating, and tends to sag rather quickly.

Newest and most dramatic on the outdoor furniture scene are the fibreglass and all-plastic ranges. Moulded fibreglass is weatherproof, light-weight and providing its design is not too rigid, extremely comfortable. It can be white or coloured, although the colour range is somewhat limited, and is priced on a par with the best timber furniture. There is some moulded plastic furniture available, which tends to be in the same idiom as fibreglass, though not as resistant to wear and tear. More intriguing is the blow-up plastic, which comes in all manner of shapes and sizes, and can be fun right in the pool as well as by the side. It must be treated with care, however, as to pierce the surface usually ruins the chair, and it should not be used where the wind is likely to send it scudding.

In deference to their comfort and pertinence in a garden setting, a special word should be said here on hammocks. Where they were once a makeshift form of bedding for troops on the march, they have now become a rather more sophisticated item of furniture. Nylon and leather webbing has replaced the original string, and tasselled cords the hemp ties. Or sometimes hammocks are made of gay canvas with shiny chrome fittings, and slung on a free-standing frame, complete with sun shade. All in all, the modern hammock is a most attractive piece of equipment, and has even more of the intrinsic comfort which has always been its particular forte.

Furniture which is made for outside is also the best kind to use for pool houses, pool enclosures, and indoor pools. Although furniture in covered areas is not subject to the same extremes of climate as that which

Grouped around a marble-topped table a Victorian cast-iron bench and modern aluminium chairs provide an inviting sitting-out place. The irregularly paved terrace is bounded by a low wall and potted plants

Shade, comfortable chairs and a small table are prerequisites for outdoor entertaining and can be achieved in the smallest of town gardens

is permanently exposed, it still has to contend with moist conditions and the greater wear and tear which everything in a casual setting must withstand.

In any terrace setting, there is much to be said for built-in furniture – concrete, stone, brick or timber. Once benches, banquettes, seats and tables are permanently in position, they require virtually no maintenance, and can be made comfortable with the addition of cushions and mattresses. This also allows for the creation of interesting bowers and niches, but take care when placing these fixtures that conversation and eating groups can be comfortably organized. One of the best ideas, if you are going to build in terrace furniture, is to focus the seating arrangement on a central table, or even a barbecue, either at normal table height or sunken to pit depth.

Colour is very important when choosing furniture for outdoor use, for here, you are dealing not just with a few pre-determined decorative accents, but the whole spectrum of nature. It is a matter of individual preference whether you choose patterned or plain fabrics, and whether you contrast or blend basic furnishing colours with those of the terrace; but try to complement nature by using garden colours in their more subtle tones. Colours which are too strident can destroy the intrinsic decorative elements which are the particular contribution of an outdoor setting.

There is a point worth noting about tables for use outdoors. While they should be of a suitable height at which to eat comfortably, they should also be usable in more general circumstances, for drinks, coffee etc. Usually, chairs for outdoor use are lower than normal, and tables to match are designed accordingly, but it may be that the chairs and tables you choose do not match. In this instance, bear in mind that 24 ins is a good height for an outdoor table, and buy your seating to suit this height.

Part of the pleasure of eating outdoors is being able to cook outdoors as well. Barbecues come in many shapes and sizes, and can be as simple as a stone-lined pit with a grill, or as elaborate as one of the complete ceramic barbecue tables produced by some continental manufacturers. In between, there is a style to suit most needs, either portable or built-in. Fixed barbecues can be built of concrete, stone or bricks, although materials which are jointed with mortar are more likely to be affected by heat than a slab concrete structure. They should be sited well away from any delicate plants which might be damaged by heat, and so that the prevailing wind does not blow smoke towards the diners. Such a barbecue should also incorporate a shelf or table on which to stand food, and possibly a basic brick oven in which to keep food warm. A mechanical or manual spit is also a useful and easily constructed addition. The advantage of a portable barbecue is that it can be moved around, not only from terrace to picnic spot, but also out of the wind, into shade or sunshine, and stored when not in use. Most are made of lightweight aluminium, though cast iron, used for the Japanese satay-style barbecues, has the advantage of being an excellent heat conductor. Charcoal and compound solid fuels are suitable for barbecue use, although there is nothing quite as good as an aromatic wood, which seems to impart a special flavour to food.

Once you have established the basic function and decorative elements of your outdoor living area, extending its uses and implanting your own particular stamp on it are largely a matter of imagination. If, for instance, the terrace is going to be a playground for young children, a corner devoted

Opposite Furniture and plant containers in glistening white polyester on an ivy-walled terrace in Paris. Chairs have easily removable cushion-covering and the table is compartmentalized, a decorative and practical arrangement

Below Cane provides a variety of garden furniture – hanging chair, stool and chair pictured here are extremely comfortable when cushioned. The small table is fitted with shelf, bottle compartments and a handle for easy carrying

to a sand pit is a worthwhile investment. This can be allowed for during the initial paving, by leaving a suitable excavation, cementing the bottom, and banking the sides with bricks. Alternatively, the sand pit can be a large, flat wooden box, or one of the plastic-lined canvas pits available ready-made. With the addition of a swing, and perhaps a climbing frame, the terrace then takes on the additional scope of a total entertainment centre for children as well as adults.

Great pleasure can be had also by encouraging birds to come to your terrace. A bird-bath – a large shell, or a water-filled urn can be as attractive as any standard design – makes a good starting point, and coupled with a feeding tray of some kind, or even a dovecote, will bring birds flocking all year round. You may even wish to go to the extent of building an aviary on your terrace; this is easily accomplished, and certainly there could be no more appropriate setting.

Flares have been mentioned previously as an alternative form of lighting, where electricity is not readily accessible. Even if you do not need them, flares can be most decorative on summer evenings (practical, too, as they will keep mosquitos and other insects at bay) and well worth adding if the terrace will be used often after sundown.

Although one tends to think of them as suitable only for large, formal gardens, constructions such as rose bowers and arches, gazebos, pavillions, summer houses and tents will give a special charm to almost any setting. All are available in pre-fabricated form, although custom made structures obviously achieve greater effects. Tents, especially, are worth considering for roof-gardens, as they are comparatively lightweight, yet offer excellent wind protection.

One fairly recent innovation which sun enthusiasts might like to consider, especially for poolside use, is the solar reflector. This is a large walled but unroofed cabinet, lined with special reflective material, with flexible sides that can be directed to follow the sun, thus halving the time it takes to acquire a good sun tan.

Swimming pools, as well as terraces, can be the focus of many original ideas. Apart from the many air mattresses, floats, duckboards and kickboards which are designed to make life afloat even more relaxing, it is possible to go several steps further. Fixed tables are easily incorporated in pools, formed in concrete during the initial building, and rising to just above water height, so that bathers do not even need to come out of the water to eat and drink. An alternative means to the same end is a floating wooden raft, anchored to the side of the pool. Fountains, too, have their special entertainment value, as well as decorative appeal, and a set of water polo goals can liven the swimming season for the whole family.

The pressures of modern living make privacy and leisure of increasing value, and lead us to appreciate more and more the time we can spend in a peaceful outdoor environment. So remember, however you plan your pool or terrace, to use discrimination, so that an outdoor environment always remains just that.

Built-in barbecue on the far side of the pool gives outdoor eating a special attraction. The terrace is sufficiently wide for table and chairs to be easily accommodated

Index